Healing Through Movement: Getting Up After a Broken Heart

By

Crista Gambrell, PhD, LPC, CPT

Dedication

To everyone, casual and close, who played a role in my healing journey, I thank you. To all the women who shared their stories of resilience with me, I stand with you. And to all the brokenhearted who aren't sure if you'll laugh again, smile again, hope again, or love again, this is for you. Put your trust in the One who sees the end from the beginning and promises to make all things beautiful in His time.

Contents

Introduction

It's taken me almost five years. It's taken that long because I really didn't want to tell this story. I didn't want this to be my thing. I didn't want this to be what I was known for. Yet, here I am, about to share some of the deepest personal pain I've endured to date—the pain of being jilted.

Part of it was that I didn't want to be seen as exploiting what happened. Sure, there are plenty of people that have no qualms about using personal tragedy to build their career platform. I'm not one of them. Nor am I one who enjoys sympathy. I want no one's pity. I have some pride and I don't want to be seen as weak. And parts of my story are just that…weak, pathetic, and nothing short of humiliating. Sometimes I'll be a character you root for. Other times I might annoy you, make you shake your head, or look the other way. But I take the risk of sharing anyway for this simple reason. When I was at my lowest and wanted to give up, like close my eyes and never wake again, give up, I had a vision of you. That's right, gentle reader. I saw you among a sea of others who had been hurt just like me. I knew I had to rise up again because if I didn't, who would give you hope?

Some of you might be wondering what the dramatic set up is all about. Breakups happen. They never feel good. Get over it, right? Well, yes

and no. Breakups are a very common and very painful human experience. We often make the decision to end romantic connections for various reasons. Try as we might, human relationships are wrought with misunderstanding, disappointments, and yes, hurt feelings and heartbreaks. Even the most well-meaning of us inevitably fall short in love and benevolence, and we both experience and cause hurt to our neighbors.

I've seen this professionally. I'm a licensed professional counselor. I've studied and practiced within the field of counseling for ten years now. One of the main reasons people come to me is because they are struggling in their relationships. For a lot of reasons, people have a hard time giving and receiving love in a healthy way. I'd later realize though that it's one thing to know something intellectually and another to know it experientially. But we'll get to that.

The thing is that usually, breakups are usually not single events, but rather they are process of engaging in termination behaviors.[1] So, a breakup might include withdrawing and avoiding, getting third parties involved in ending the relationship, communicating about relationship dissatisfaction, and ultimately expressing the desire to breakup.[2] But sometimes there are brutal endings that you don't see coming. There are breakups that shake you to your core.

When breakups are sudden or unexpected, they can produce intense reactions that mimic post-traumatic stress in some.[3] They are so much more than just misunderstanding or normal relationship fallout. They're a violent assault on your soul.

That was the kind of ending I had.

It nearly broke me. I certainly felt broken in the process. The reality, however, was that although I felt hard pressed on every side, I was never crushed. I was perplexed but not in despair. I was persecuted but not abandoned, and though the experience struck me down, I was not destroyed (2 Corinthians 4:7-9).

So, here I am having lived to tell my story…a story that I hope encourages you. There are lots of approaches I could take to telling it. I could write the story as a counselor. Because I am. I could write it as a Ph.D. researcher. Because I am. But, I don't want to. I mean, sure, it would be emotionally easier for me to assume a clinical or scholarly distance. But I would be doing a disservice to me and you. I want you to know if you ever come into my office for counseling the reason I can perfectly reflect your pain is not because I can imagine it or I've read about it. I have felt it. And even if you never come to me for counseling, I want you to know that beyond the smile, beyond the credentials, beyond any outward markers of success, is a girl like you who had her heart broken, obliterated really, and who experienced healing as well.

This is what this book is about. It's about the process of getting up, not merely the pain of falling down. This is the story of a girl. A girl who was jilted by a dear love. Her first (and so far only) love. A girl who was rejected and humiliated. A girl who wanted to die and was almost down for the count, yet resurrected into a fierce warrior of a woman. I'll share why breakups hurt so much. I'll also share the stories of other women I interviewed that suffered similar cutoffs and arose from the ashes. This is my story, our story, of recovering joy and healing through movement

Boys are Mean

*Un-break my heart, say you love me again. Undo this hurt you
caused when you walked out the door and walked out of my life.*

– Toni Braxton, "Un-Break My Heart"[4]

While I don't have extensive experience with dating or
relationships, my breakups have been doozies. So much so that I
am always genuinely baffled by people who are friends with their
ex. You know those weirdos who wish their ex nothing but the best
and all that. Clearly, these people haven't experienced gladiator-
style blood bath endings like I have. My attitude toward the
handful of exes I have is much more like Miranda Hobbes from
Sex and the City. "We didn't work out. You need to not exist."[5]
Here's why.

Growing up, I was really quiet and a little socially
awkward. The whole world of dating and liking boys was always
intimidating to me. I think I had a couple of boyfriends in middle
school, which I'm pretty sure only lasted a week, if that. Those

relationships consisted of a few phone calls, walks to class, and a couple of uncomfortable kisses. When I think about my first real boyfriend that I actually went on dates with, he didn't come along until ninth grade. We'll call him Tim.

Tim and I were an unlikely pair. We met in band. I was the shy, slight clarinet player and Tim was the bad boy who stood over six feet tall and weighed about 250 lbs. Oh and he honest-to-goodness had a voice like James Earl Jones. I'm not sure what that boy ate, but Tim looked like a thirty-year-old bouncer instead of the fifteen-year-old tuba player he was.

Well, we started talking and then we eventually started dating. It went as well as you might imagine for two teenagers that really had nothing in common other than liking each other. Around the three-month mark we started fighting about stupid stuff. I can't even tell you what our last fight was about. I'm sure I was pouting about something and he was being insensitive in response.

3

Whatever it was, little did I know that it would be the beginning of the end.

Due to our class schedules, I knew I wouldn't see him again until after fourth period. We usually walked together to fifth period since our classes were in the same building. But that day, he didn't wait for me. Instead, he walked to class with another girl.

I immediately felt panicked. I had planned to talk to him and apologize, but he was clearly still upset. I didn't want to lose my composure, so I just tried to walk fast to catch up with him. I started to lose him, so I called his name. He kept walking. I called it again, this time much louder so there was no way he didn't hear it. He kept on walking. When others noticed, they busted out laughing at how he completely ignored me. Meanwhile, I felt my face burn bright red and the tears I had been swallowing down burst forth uncontrollably. It felt like I had the wind knocked out of me.

For the rest of the day, fifth period English, sixth period P.E., I cried...sobbed. I didn't care who saw. I couldn't stop the flood gates. I cried the entire bus ride home. I cried when I got home. I went out to dinner to one of those cafeteria-style restaurants with my mom and her friend and I cried there too. What had I done? What could've been so awful that it would've warranted ignoring my existence? That was the kind of questioning I did for days to come as Toni Braxton's "Un-Break My Heart" and Mary J. Blige's "Not Gon' Cry" tormented me by playing non-stop on the radio.

That, my friends, was my first breakup. Yes, it was high school. I was needy and emotionally immature. He was callous and emotionally immature. But let me tell you, that image of him walking away as I cried out for him stuck with me throughout high school and most of college. My take home? I learned that boys are mean to me and then they leave. And not just mean, but a kick the dog, unnecessary kind of mean. I even swore off dating for years. I

5

rationalized that it was important to focus on my education and spiritual growth. But really, it was that mental image from high school of being so obviously rejected, in front of others no less, that kept me from opening up like that again. It was so disgraceful that I wanted to be sure I never went through that again. Little did I know I would go through it again and it would be significantly worse.

The Breakup Part I: Dear John

When all else fails just say what happened.

– Elizabeth Gilbert, author of *Eat, Pray, Love* and *Big*

Magic[6]

I appreciate simplicity. I guess if I'm going to self-disclose in a book I might as well jump right in, huh? But let me preface it by saying, I'm not going to get into super specific detail for two reasons. 1) Because I don't want you to miss the forest for the trees. Sometimes an overemphasis on someone else's story detail and timeline can keep you from connecting it with your own. 2) Even though it's been almost five years from the time of this publication, parts of the story are still tender. So, in the name of not drowning in a puddle of tears and delaying this book any further, let me just share enough of what needs to be shared, so we can get to the redemption. Sound like a plan?

As you might expect, names and a few details have been altered to protect those involved. The ex? We'll call him Lucifer. Just kidding.

How about another high ranking angel? Michael. That gives you an image of how I saw him. I met Michael in college, but we didn't attend at the same time. He was a good deal older than me and was really more like a spiritual guide/mentor. I had a school-girl type of crush on him for a long time. He seemed perfect. He was a safe, mature man who knew all of my anxieties about guys. He was strong, yet sensitive. He was spiritual, yet down-to-earth. He was dark and handsome and yet humble too. Basically, he was everything I ever wanted. I never imagined anything would realistically happen. He happened to be totally unavailable…partly because of the age difference and the mentor role.

But mainly because he belonged to someone else. That made him completely off-limits and therefore, safe. I believed that we could be friends without any expectation of romance.

So, when he affectionately called me pet names, it didn't feel creepy or inappropriate at all. I knew it was intimate. Sure. But it felt platonic, paternal even. It felt like I was incredibly special and that meant so much to me.

9

As our friendship deepened over the years and he confided in me about his relationship dissatisfaction, I didn't understand at the time that people who intend to cheat play both sides. In my early twenties, I was naïve to the notion of eliciting sympathy and grooming the other person you want to become involved with... Putting feelers out there to see how they respond. I was just honored that he trusted me so much. Like I said, he was my mentor, but it felt good to be his counselor. I saw it as a good sign that he felt comfortable to open up to me. So many people relied on him. I wanted him to know he could rely on me.

If you're reading this, you know exactly where it's going. Even as I write it several years later, it's so much more obvious to me now than it was then. We got emotionally involved first and then he eventually pursued me romantically. I felt like I won the lottery. From the first expression of feelings to the time we were ready to move forward in our future, it was about four years. That's a lot of time invested for a girl in her twenties. Even though he still wasn't free to pursue me, he did. And although I never thought I'd find myself in that situation, I was. Young, dumb, and head over heels in love...in love with a man who belonged to someone else.

It took a while, but in time, he did end his other relationship. I rationalized that it wasn't a problem to become involved prematurely because I was the one he was always meant to be with. I believed that because that's what he told me and because it's what I desperately needed to hear. I reasoned that even though it wasn't an ideal beginning, God was going to give us a beautiful ending. Like I said, young, dumb, and head over heels in love.

Let's fast-forward a bit. After some time of dating long distance, I finally got a job in the state where he lived and I relocated. Even though I was head over heels, I was being sensible. I didn't move until I got a job. I wanted my own place, rather than living in his. Plus, I was so close to getting everything I ever wanted. I could almost hear wedding bells. It wouldn't be much longer, I was certain. Little did I know, but things were about to take a drastic turn.

I was home visiting family for Thanksgiving. He wasn't able to join me this time. Admittedly, he seemed a little off the week before. Even his goodbye to me at the airport seemed a little distant, but I didn't think anything of it. He had given me a white gold diamond promise ring in October for my birthday. Noting that my birthday is in October is significant and you'll see why. Michael took my hands, looked in my eyes, and said, "You know I want to marry you, right?" Then, he placed the ring on my finger. The LEFT ring finger, ya'll. I remember beaming. Our relationship had been years in the making and now we were about to live happily ever after. I'm certain that last sentence made all my feminist readers cringe. Honestly, I cringed writing it. I was a career woman. I got my Ph.D. at twenty-seven. I had a license to practice counseling in multiple states. Yet, if I'm 100% honest with myself all I wanted was to be Michael's wife.

Even though I hadn't gotten an official proposal yet, I was so sure it was coming that I started planning my wedding. After getting a promise ring, you'd get why I'd be encouraged. I had a computer file of ring cuts I liked and had already started looking at wedding dresses. My mom, sister, and I even started checking out hotel venues in my hometown. Little did I know the Thanksgiving turkey that was about to drop.

I'll never forget the call. I actually called him because something felt wrong. This is super important to realize. *Even when your mind doesn't understand, your gut will react to the flags and indicators.* On and off throughout our relationship, I had a recurring dream. I'm not a big dreamer and I certainly don't have recurring dreams. But, when I was with Michael, I did. It was always the same theme. He'd propose and I'd be thrilled, but something was always off about the ring. It either didn't fit or I

13

didn't like the cut or he'd propose but then have to leave again. Remember, the first few years we were long distance. Anyway, something was always off. But when I'd wake up, I'd just be so excited about an engagement dream that I'd ignore the other ominous details.

At any rate, over that Thanksgiving, as I was happily planning our future, I was simultaneously anxious and didn't know why. I figured when we talked he would assure me it was work stress or something. I never expected what I actually got. It went something like this.

"Hey Cris, what's up? I saw you called."

"Yeah, I'm just checking in. Something just feels off and I wanted to see if everything's ok."

"Well, actually, I was going to wait until you got back to talk about this. But...I don't want to get married, dude."

The "dude" part was charming, right? We called each other dude a lot, so normally it wouldn't have been a problem. But to

14

reference me in such a casual way while he was proceeding to break my heart? Let's just say it didn't sit well.

Silence on my end. "You don't want to marry *me* or you don't want to get married?"

Silence on his end. "I…I don't want to marry anybody…"

You know how in movies when the background noise fades, everything slows down and the character has an out-of-body experience? That's kind of what happened. I must have dissociated a little because I only remember pieces of what he said after that.

He rambled on about it not feeling right. He said something or other about the holiday apart being a test and the fact that he didn't really miss me proved that it wasn't meant to be. The details are blurry. It's like a checked out once I heard it was over.

I collapsed into sobs when we got off the phone. I talked to my mom. I called my best friend. No one could say anything to me. I was inconsolable. I called him back repeatedly. It wasn't very dignified, I well know, but I was desperate. It felt like my

15

world was crashing down and I had to hang on for dear life. When he wouldn't pick up, I texted him angrily that he owed me a conversation.

"No, Cris. You need time to get used to this."

It was a slap in the face. It was tuba Tim ignoring me in the hallway in high school all over again. Forget Mary J's just-be-a-gangster-and-deal-with-it approach in her song "Not Gon' Cry." This was a Jordin Sparks &

> **"Tell me how I'm supposed to breathe with no air. Can't live, can't breathe with no air. It's how I feel when I know you ain't there."**
>
> **- Jordin Sparks & Chris Brown, "No Air"**

Chris Brown "No Air" moment. I was a basket case and could hardly breathe.

[7]Perhaps there are no good times to end a relationship. But I will say for those of you thinking about parting ways with your partner, the holidays are the worst time. There are the obvious reasons like family coming together and celebrating. That's hard to

16

do when you're bleeding inside. I remember forcing myself to be with family for an hour or so at a time, but then needing to step away to cry again. Everyone knew what had happened. Graciously though, they gave me space.

I think the worst part of that holiday season was the engagement commercials. You're probably familiar with the Kay's Jewelers jingle "Every Kiss Begins with Kay". Every time it aired and I heard that stupid jingle, it felt like I was being mocked. I was the silly girl who had put her hope in a promise ring, believing it would be exchanged for an engagement ring. It looked like that wasn't going to happen. Instead of a ring, I got a "Dear John letter"…or phone call, as it were. I felt like a fool.

I got through the weekend and I flew back home- home being where I had relocated to be with him. It had only been five months since I moved away from family and friends to start a new life. Now, I was flying back to a life that had been suddenly ripped away. A fresh wave of grief hit. As a leaned my head back in my seat on the plane and let new tears fall, a picture came to mind. I saw an image of a paper and pencil. What was written on the paper was being erased and something new was being written. I believed that was a message from God—this particular ending was over, but that didn't mean the story was over. A new story was being written for me. Before I could get to it though, I would have to walk through a very dark winter.

Post-it

It's in not *having the difficult conversation that makes you the bad guy.*

— Carrie Bradshaw, *Sex and the City*[8]

In *Sex and the City*, Sarah Jessica Parker's character, Carrie, was dumped by her boyfriend, Berger. Actually, what happened was after saying he wanted to work things out the night before, she awakens the next morning to a post-it note with these words: *I can't. I'm sorry. Don't hate me.* Then, the whole episode is about her trying to move on from a breakup of such poor form.

Later that night she's at the club with her girls and she runs into Berger's friends. She proceeds to get into a bit of an argument with them when they appear to defend his cowardly departure because there's "no good way to end a relationship." Carrie, with a raised voice, tells them off.

She explains that women just want an ending that's dignified and decent and honors the time spent together. She reasons with them that there are any number of ways to do that, "That DO NOT involve a post-it!!"[9]

If you haven't seen that episode, check it out because it's really funny. It does a great job of making an awful situation humorous. I can tell you from experience though that in real life, it's not funny at all. Bad breakups only add insult to injury. That's a big reason why I did a formal qualitative study about it. I went through my university's Institutional Review Board. I did an extensive literature review and designed my research methodology. I placed a call for participants to interview. Why? Because I desperately needed to know I wasn't alone. I needed to know that it wasn't just my experience either. I learned after speaking to the sample of thirteen women that I wasn't alone. As they shared their breakup stories, they echoed similar sentiments. Here's how some of theirs went.

He just texted me. He didn't even call me.

He called me up one night, completely cold and uncaring

and broke up with me over the phone.

What people should realize is that indirectness makes things so much worse. Like the Carrie told Berger's friends, "It's in *no*t having the difficult conversation that makes you the bad guy." Indirect termination strategies are considered as some of the least compassionate ways of ending a relationship.[10] Not offering closure face to face is generally less empathetic because it has more to do with minimizing the initiator's personal distress rather than considering another's pain. Breakups are generally difficult for both parties, but typically the psychological advantage rests with the initiators. They have had time to mentally prepare for life without their partner. So, when ending a relationship, the one who wants out can be selfish or considerate of someone else's pain.[11]

What might be even worse than just a poorly executed ending is learning of infidelity. Several women I interviewed

22

learned their partner cheated on them, which led to the ending.
Here are their stories.

I looked at his phone when he was outside and saw an

inappropriate conversation with a woman he worked with.

I never considered his character to be in question until I

found out he was married at his home base.

He replaced me immediately. Like I'm sure it was within a

few weeks he was dating this new person, if it hadn't

started before.

There's a saying: "Comedy is tragedy plus time." Like I

said, that *Sex and the City* episode was hilarious. I now see that it

was probably so smartly written because one or more of the writers

had experienced a poor form breakup. Perhaps they were

completely ignored, tuba player-Tim style or maybe they had their

own holiday "Dear John" call. There's no denying those are pretty

bad ways to part ways. But you could reason they were just scared,

immature, and didn't know what they wanted. Unfortunately, for me, I would later learn that there was more to it all than just that.

And if I could've chosen between a post-it ending and what

actually happened, I would've chosen the post-it.

Breakup Part II: Barely Breathing

'Cause I am barely breathing. I can't find the air. Don't know who

I'm kidding imagining you care.

— Duncan Sheik, "Barely Breathing"[12]

I wish I could say that was the worst of it…that he got cold feet, decided we were better as friends, and just wanted to end things amicably before they went any farther. As much as that would hurt, that would fall under the category of a normal breakup though, and as I said before, that's not what I had. Over the next three months, the truth came out and it was worse than I anticipated.

For the first few weeks after he ended it, we didn't really talk. Other than a courtesy call after I flew back in apologizing for how it ended, we weren't in touch. Like he said, I needed time to get used to the idea that it was over. That was difficult though as I was still in the bargaining phase of grief. He was the only reason I moved to that area. He was my only friend. We lived in the same

26

apartment complex because I wanted to be close to him. Plus, we had years together. I wasn't willing to accept that it was over. No. This just had to be cold feet. We would ease back into a friendship and then find our way back together for sure.

That's what we did, the first part at least. We started hanging out again and he was warm. He would smile and it would both relieve and confuse me. Was he looking at me with eyes of love again, or was he just being friendly? After gathering with friends, I decided to ask him. I wrote him a long email pretty much saying I still loved him and still wanted to be with him. No surprises there on my end. But his reply was one I never saw coming. He shared all the ways I hadn't met his needs in the relationship. He shared his hurt and frustration and the ways I didn't measure up. This hit me like a ton of bricks. He had never indicated dissatisfaction. I knew there had to be more to the story. This would take more than an email or phone call. I begged him to come over. He reluctantly agreed. I was anxious but hopeful. Now that he was finally giving me reasons, maybe we could work on them. We could fix it.

As soon as I saw him, I could tell his guard up. All the warmth was gone. It was like he was annoyed. He proceeded to tell me he was never in love with me and I was never *The One*. He wanted me to be, but realized I wasn't. Mind you, this was after years of being called *bella* and *beloved*. This was after being placed on a pedestal and all but worshiped for being *the only one for him* and *perfectly made for him*. Now, I was *like a sister* to him. He even added that that's why he never wanted to take me out on dates. This one really stung. I mean, yeah, we normally hung around the house, but I thought it was because we were homebodies. We'd cook dinner and drink wine. It was a nice time. Plus, we were saving money. I would never have guessed he just didn't want to spend time in public with me. But that's what he so kindly shared with me…how he had tickets for events and concerts, but just didn't want to take me.

"I didn't want to go. It didn't feel right."

Like I said, that one really got me.

> **"Sugar your heart has been broken. But I can still see true love shine in your eyes."**
>
> **– Kem, "Why Won't you Stay?"**

[13]I searched his eyes for the truth. Was he pushing me away because he was scared? Guys do that, I later learned. Well, not just guys, but anyone who's broken. The bigger the ass they can be in the end, the better. If you hate them, you'll get over them more easily and they don't feel as bad for pushing you away like that. The thing was that I didn't hate him and I wasn't going to let him make me. I loved him.

I tried to appeal to his empathetic nature, so I told him I was looking for wedding venues with my family over Thanksgiving. His response? He winced sarcastically. The kind of sucks-to-be-you face you might make while watching *America's*

Funniest Home Videos or a bobsled team careen into the side of the track. How could he not care? Was he seriously amused by my pain? Now, he was just being mean. Kick the dog unnecessary kind of mean.

He said all of these things so matter-of-fact. It was like he was stating a simple truth that should've been blatantly apparent to me had my eyes been open to the signs. But it wasn't apparent to me at all. Was he rewriting history to validate his choice? Or were there signs that I had blindly missed?

There were a couple of times in elementary school that uncoordinated me attempted to play kickball. One time the ball hit me dead and center in my chest and knocked the wind out of me. It was probably a total of three seconds before I finally caught my breath and let out a wail. But in that moment, it felt like time had slowed down and I was dying a slow death. That was kickball, but this conversation felt a lot like it. Instead of an actual ball coming at me, I had been violently kicked off Michael's pedestal, put in a

30

sister box in his mind, and there was no going back. Once again, I could hardly breathe.

He went on to say he still had feelings for a random ex. It was a relationship he had many years before. Apparently, he had always felt bad for blowing it with her. He felt like he needed to see what could happen with her and there was no way he could marry me if he still wondered about someone else. Again, I was hearing what he said, but still not taking it all in. I was supposed to be the one. I was supposed to be *bella*. I was supposed to be legitimate. How could he rip me of that title and so easily give it to someone else? He had to be delusional. This was a midlife crisis or something. I told you he was a lot older than me. This had to be a midlife psychosis of some sort and I was concerned for him. I reasoned that even if he did track down his mystery ex from his twenties, what kind of woman would respond favorably to some guy from her past initiating a relationship out of the blue? Perhaps he was crazy, but I was still very naïve.

31

A few weeks later I learned that they had reconnected and were talking again, which made me think something was going on before he ended things with me. Then, a few weeks after that, I learned that she moved in. You didn't know you were in for some *Telemundo* type twists, huh? Well, me either. Not only did I have to swallow down the jagged little pill of him not wanting me and instead pursing someone else; I got to watch him move on right in front of me. They were living together just a short two-minute walk from me. I moved to get married and he had the nerve to play house right in front of me. This nightmare had gone from bad to worse and I couldn't wake up from it.

Fight, Flight, or Freeze

There's a side to you that I never knew, never knew and the things

you'd say they were never true, never true.

– Adele, "Set Fire to the Rain"[14]

As you can see from my story, you get why I would've

opted for the post-it. It was a sequence of events that drove the

dagger further and further into my heart and then twisting it a little

more for good measure. The Thanksgiving phone breakup. The

acknowledgment of dissatisfaction that had not been previously

expressed. Admitting there was, in fact, another woman. And then

learning that they were playing house next door and even

discussing marriage. It was too much to bear.

With each revelation I'd lose sleep for days. I'd toss and

turn not wanting to believe any of this was real. About a week after

each bomb dropped, I would finally start to get a few hours of

sleep again. I'd get a break from the pain only to have it come back

like a flood when I woke up. In my dreams, we would reconcile.

34

He was repentant. We were together and working it out. Then, my eyes would open to a new day, I'd remember everything again, and I would weep. That happened every day for months.

You can imagine why I had thoughts of falling asleep and not waking up.

I scheduled a physical on Valentine's Day that year. It was reminiscent of Tina Fey's *30 Rock* character, Liz, scheduling a root canal in personal protest to Valentine's Day. Another funny show and another funny character. Except again, real life isn't nearly as funny as TV. I took the day off from work because I wanted a total day to myself without any triggers of that God-forsaken love day or Michael and his new girlfriend being intimate. Instead, the doctor seemed like a reasonable place to be.

I got a full workup for no other reason than I wanted to make sure I wasn't dying. It sounds dramatic, but it seriously felt like I was dying. It's weird. When the very worst thing you imagine actually happens to you, then anything awful enters the realm of conceivability. Nothing feels safe anymore. To my surprise, although it probably shouldn't have been, I learned that my systolic blood pressure (the top number) was 142.

I don't recall the bottom number at the moment. But to give you an idea, 120/80 or lower is consider normal and I was well above that into the hypertensive range. At twenty-nine years old! Oh and my fasting glucose readings were at 126, the diabetic range.

Normal is considered any value at 100 or less. I couldn't believe it. I had never had health issues before. I wasn't overweight. I wasn't inactive. I was traumatized and my body was reacting as if my very life had been threatened. It had in my eyes.

This was too much. Heartbroken is one thing. High blood pressure and potential health problems are another. I felt like I was going crazy. Was I being dramatic? Or was it really as bad as it seemed to me? As it turns out, I wasn't alone. The majority of women I spoke to had similar strong reactions after their breakups.

Every woman I spoke to reacted to the loss physically, emotionally, and mentally. They each reported a disturbance in sleeping and eating right after the breakup.

I had intense anxiety and heart pain over the loss of him and our relationship.

I had a panic attack. I couldn't breathe and I was hyperventilating and turned white, I could barely function, I cried hysterically nonstop for a week.

I was in shock and disbelief- how can the person who is closest to you do something so hurtful? I felt like the floor had been pulled out from underneath me…like someone hit me in the chest and then sucked all the energy/life out of me.

I was in shock. I couldn't wrap my mind around the betrayal…was so blindsided.

I couldn't stop thinking about her and him kissing and being intimate…It was horrible.

37

This was more than just an unfortunate case of hurt feelings. This was more than the typical grief or disappointment that follow a breakup. This was a targeted attack and one that was significant enough to cause traumatic stress reactions in us. As it turns out, these are pretty common reactions to infidelity.[15] Re-experiencing, avoidance, and increased arousal—they're, unfortunately, pretty normal.[16] Just think about it. When you're settling into what you believe is your happily ever after, only to have it ripped away…when you're secure in your identity as someone's one and only and then you're abruptly replaced, that's enough to leave even the strongest, most secure woman pretty rattled.

Here's the thing though. Infidelity is just one type of relational transgression.

Rejection is another type and can include abandonment, unreciprocated romantic overtures, jilting, or lack of interest in maintaining a given relationship.[17] For at least half the women I spoke to, their partner was not known to be unfaithful, but they still wanted to end things. The partners were described as ambivalent and unwilling to fully commit. When their partners finally decided to leave instead of fight to make it work, it left these women questioning everything, including their worth.

Back to the blood pressure reading and the Valentine's Day physical. Yes, I was in my feelings about everything for a while. Given how things went down, I earned the time to weep, wail, and nurse my wounds. Then something happened. I got pissed. When I considered my ex's actions, how incredulous, how despicable, how egregious they were, a rage like I had never felt before consumed me. What I call an "Oh, hell no!" fury burned within me. It was time to fight. I wasn't fighting Michael though. I was fighting for my life. I was fighting for my happy ending that he attempted to steal from me. I was fighting for my dignity, my redemption, and my vindication.

[18]They say you don't necessarily choose how you'll react to a threatening situation. The fight, flight, or freeze response is said to be biologically predetermined. But your initial reaction doesn't matter as much as your next. My next step was to take my life back.

> "There's a fire starting in my heart reaching a fever pitch and it's bringing me out the dark."
>
> – Adele, "Rolling in the Deep"

Things are Bad, but God is Good

You survived the worst of times. God was always on your

side.

— Donald Lawrence, "Seasons"[19]

This is sometimes difficult for people to understand. But when you are going through a trial or difficulty, that's not the time to learn a new skill set. It's really hard to develop brand new coping skills once you're in battle. All you have to fight with is whatever is already in your arsenal. When you're emotionally flooded and feeling pulled on all sides there's no way you even have the wherewithal to pick up new tools. You must draw on your internal reserve and hope it's enough to get you through. Mine was my faith.

I grew up in the church and had always been a good girl for all intents and purposes. My mom was pretty strict, so I wasn't allowed to do a lot of what other kids could do. Everyone expected me to go crazy once I got to college, but it was quite the opposite.

My faith deepened. I don't want to paint a picture of perfection because I was and am not, not by any stretch of the imagination. My heart and love for God were sincere though and I believed very idealistically, that if you follow a certain formula, you'll get the right results. Real life, however, taught me in the most unpleasant of ways that that's not at all how it works.

You might think that I would've gotten mad at God when things fell apart, that it would've shaken my faith. I had believed so much that my Michael was the one and our relationship was destined. God had opened the door for me to relocate. He'd given me a job and a place to live. Despite obstacles early on in the relationship, we had worked through them and had a supportive group of friends and family rooting for us. If it wasn't going to work out in the long run, why would it be allowed to work out at all? Why wasn't I spared from the heartache and shame? I suppose those are normal questions to ask. Maybe on some level I did wonder about them. But for some reason, not once did I blame or curse God. I knew this wasn't His doing. I knew He wasn't in the business of destruction.

When you're going through something hard, faith gets really simple. It's not about mental ascent or deep theology. You don't get all philosophical about the nature and meaning of life. You get down to barebones truth.

> "He sees the tears you cry. He shares your pain inside. Sometimes you wonder why He allows you to go through what you go through."
>
> — Marvin Sapp, "He Has His Hands on You"

For me, that was God is good and God is love. These were truths imparted in my childhood. Certainly, I had advanced beyond that understanding as I walked with God. But when I was stripped of everything, those truths were what I clung to. That was all that mattered.

[20]I surrounded myself with worship music. I have always loved music, especially gospel and inspirational. But it really

became my lifeline then. I remember playing Marvin Sapp's "He Has His Hand on You" on repeat. It was one of many songs I played repeatedly just to encourage my soul that I was being held and I wasn't abandoned. I clung to promises from the scriptures that "He is close to the brokenhearted and saves those who are crushed in spirit" (Psalm 34:18), and "The sacrifices of God are a broken spirit; a broken and contrite heart He won't despise" (Psalm 51:17). And you know what? It was a sacrifice to worship at that time.

When your heart is bleeding and bruised, the last thing you want to do is sing or pray or declare goodness in a situation. It hurts to even speak. But in that gritty place of raw emotion, that's when your faith is made known. That's when you realize who God really is to you.

Understanding God's nature helped me separate out man's actions from His. Knowing how much God loved me, I knew there was no way He would see me destroyed and broken but still bless

45

and prosper my ex. I knew if He was a good father, the only one I'd ever known, He wouldn't sit idly back without making the wrong situations right. It wasn't about revenge, although if I'm honest, it was, at first. It was about learning to trust that whatever situation a man intended for my harm, God would use for my good. That's the beauty of redemption- no matter how messed up the situation is He makes all things beautiful in its time.

When you begin to see life through this lens, then you develop resilience. It didn't matter that my father wasn't in the picture. It didn't even matter that Michael ended things in such a cowardly, cruel way. Man's shortcomings do not change God's nature and they certainly don't alter your destiny.

It's hard but you must not change your theology based on a season of suffering. There are unshakable, infallible truths that you must cling to no matter what the circumstances are. He is good and what He does it good. He knows the plans He has for you and they're plans to prosper and not harm you. My faith was strengthened so much during that time that I even found myself making this personal recommitment to God:

Lord, I know you are able and willing to deliver me. But even if you don't, I will bow down to no other. For my life is not my own. It was purchased by your blood. And I no longer live unto myself. I belong to and live for you. I would have despaired and lost all hope had I not believed I would see your goodness in the land of the living. Therefore, I choose to wait for you, trust you, and watch how you will be good to me.

With this hope as an anchor for my soul, I was able to worship Him more deeply than ever before, knowing He is good, what He does is good, and He'll work it out for my good.

The Making of a Warrior

There's a power deep inside you, an inner strength you'll find in

time of need...the glow.

— Dwight David, "The Last Dragon"[21]

The holiday season of the breakup also happened to be the

year of Adele's amazing, but gut wrenching album, *21*. I loved her

music, but it didn't sit well with a fresh heartbreak, and certainly

not with betrayal. I knew I was going to have to get busy

distracting myself to avoid drowning in a sea of self-

pity...drowning any further, that is.

I had wanted to try martial arts for a while. Since I had

newfound time on my hands, I wanted to start right away. My

colleague, Jason, a tang soo do instructor, suggested kung fu.

Given my dance background he thought the aesthetic of the

Chinese tradition would appeal to me. After researching a few

places online, I decided to try one the same week. My first visit to

Tony Brown's Kung Fu School was on Christmas Eve.

I pulled up to the warehouse area on a Saturday morning. It didn't look like much on the outside, but I was immediately intrigued. It reminded me the cult classic and one of my all time favorite movies, *Berry Gordy's The Last Dragon*. I walked into the small gym and it was full of trophies, medals, and pictures from competitions. There were all kinds of weaponry and sparring equipment and an open floor space to workout. There was a very small group of no more than five or six total, a couple of kids, but mostly adults. After introductions and exchanging a few pleasantries, we all stood around waiting for the instructor. A few minutes later he arrived and was quite different than what I expected.

Sifu Tony was a white man in his fifties or sixties. He had a muscular build, salt and pepper hair, a warm smile, and one arm. That's right. This kung fu master that had trained extensively and continued to teach in traditional Taiwanese form only had one arm. Whether it was a difference that existed from birth or due to an accident, I soon realized he really only needed one arm to put someone on the ground. Like *The Last Dragon's* Bruce Leroy, he was more than met the eye, and I knew I was about to learn so much more than martial arts.

Class began and so did my training. For the next five months I went to the club a couple times a week. We would start with a group warm up. Sometimes we did some partner drills. But generally, we would break off into our own individual workouts. I started learning Chung I Chuan, said to be a Taiwan military form. Like many of the sequences, it looked like a beautifully choreographed dance. I preferred the individual work to the partner work. Even though everyone was nice and welcoming, I kind of just needed a space to be with others but do my own thing. For those two hours or so each week, I was able to get lost in time and learn the skills of fighting. And I desperately needed to fight. Life had given me a cruel blow and I needed find a way to stand up again and tap into my power. Here are some lessons I learned during my time with Sifu Tony.

Never Fight in Someone's Style Unless You're Better than Them

This has to do with effort qualities. If someone approaches you strong and direct, change your approach by becoming fluid and indirect. The reverse is true as well. It's really a matter of balance. It's like the yin yang principle. If you approach them in the same way and they're better or stronger than you, then you'll lose. If you come a different way, more often than not, you'll diffuse the situation. The lesson here is do not fight like another person unless you know you can beat them. It would've been so easy to stoop to his level. Once I tapped into the anger, I had plenty of daydreams about inflicting physical harm, destroying property, confronting him and the new woman...you know...full-on psycho ex-girlfriend style. I knew intuitively though that would give me no traction.

He would either laugh off the anger or react defensively. That would give him more proof that I was never really the one. Instead, as vulnerable and weak as it might have seemed, I expressed hurt and deep sadness.

So, later when a mutual friend said, "You know she really loved you, right?" he was able to hear it, believe it, and it brought the necessary conviction and remorse over his behavior. It was too late to fix anything, of course, but he would have to live with trying to destroy someone who really loved him.

> **"But you didn't have to cut me off. Make out like it never happened and that we were nothing."**
>
> **– Gotye, "Somebody That I Used to Know"**

[22]Scholar First, Then a Warrior

There's a sequence called Yi Sup Lo Kuen, or 26 Fists. It's all about the scholar/warrior salute. The lesson here was to remember that we're scholars first. This concept resonated with me as soon as Sifu said it. His wisdom was this. If you can talk your way out of a conflict, do that. But never forget you're a warrior.

This was a much needed reminder that although I am gentle and prefer the path of peace, I won't hesitate to stand up and defend myself if the situation requires it. This is my secret weapon.

By nature, I am kind and accommodating. I'm diplomatic and congenial. If and when you cross me, however, I come back with force and intensity that you never saw coming.

I dig that about me. It's like that fighter side of me is a diamond and it didn't form until it was under significant pressure. I don't bring it forth all the time, only when the situation requires it.

Know Your Vulnerability

Regarding self-defense, I learned if someone grabs your arm, pull away where their hands open. That's their vulnerability. This highlights the importance of knowing your own open doors and entry points as well as your enemy's. If you know them, you can exploit them to your advantage. Without this knowledge, you're vulnerable to danger. They say hindsight is 20/20 and I definitely know that it be true. There were red flags and indicators along the way that my dream relationship wasn't destined for happily ever after. The secrecy. The power differential. Living in two different realities. In fact, if I'm honest with myself, there were problematic relational dynamics that compromised it from the very beginning as well as throughout the relationship.

But because I wasn't fully conscious of my weaknesses and unwilling to see his, it made for a traumatic ending that perhaps could've been avoided with self-awareness.

Sometimes Stillness is Harder than Movement.

Another lesson I learned was from one of the more challenging body postures. In the style of kung fu I learned, there's a stance called Mao bu, or horse stance. Essentially, it's just a squat or a lunge where you remain half seated and half standing. Sometimes we would begin class by taking this stance for upwards of ten minutes. Imagine doing a plank or a wall sit or holding any other still posture isometrically for as long as you can. It's a test of endurance. In an interesting parallel, I couldn't just flee the situation, as much as I might have wanted to. I had a lease. I had a job. I had clients who depended on me. Even though I was triggered every single day during that winter and spring, I couldn't immediately remove myself from the situation. As painful and insufferable as it was, I had to be still and endure.

Don't Let Anyone Steal Your Power

I believe the most profound lesson I gleaned from Sifu was a comment he made in passing one night. I don't recall which series I was learning but we were working on punches.

At some point he stopped the practice and looked me dead in my eye. I felt like he was prophesying to my soul. He said, "If you learn how to do this, you'll always be able to protect yourself. People will come up to you and then back off because they'll see something in your eyes. You'll never be a victim again." That spoke to the deepest part of me because at the time I felt like a victim. Someone I loved did something awful and I couldn't do anything about it. But as it says in Proverbs 24:16, "Though a righteous man falls seven times, he will get up." And eventually I did.

When I was overcome with grief and despair, I was immobilized. But when I tapped into my anger and indignation, I was able to stand again. I pulled it together enough to apply for jobs and get a plan in place for moving on with my life. I was not about to sit around and watch my ex seal the deal with someone else or move out of the area and desert me out of state without friends or family.

Now was the time to pave my own way. There's something strangely beautiful that happens when everything goes to hell in a hand basket. There's freedom in being stripped of everything. You can start over.

My tutelage under Sifu Tony was cut short because I got a job as a college mental health counselor and moved out of the area. I'll never forget one of my last classes though. It had just rained that Saturday morning and the sun had come out. We decided to workout outside and we witnessed a beautiful rainbow. For me, it was a clear sign. God was with me and what was meant for my destruction, God would use for my good.

I had hoped to continue with kung fu at my new location, but my schedule didn't really permit. Whether I resume it in the future or not, I will always remember Sifu who came alongside me during that season to begin my restoration to wholeness. From what I remember, Cantonese culture doesn't do goodbyes. Instead their departures roughly translate to "I will see you next time." To Sifu Tony, wherever you are, I am forever grateful. Joy gen.

From Wailing to Dancing

You turned my wailing into dancing; you removed my sackcloth

and clothed me with joy.

– Psalm 30:11

Well, by the grace of God I made it through that cold, dark winter and it was time to pack up and move on. I can still remember my friend's words echoing as my mom and I drove out of my apartment complex. "Don't look back." That simple phrase was pregnant with so much meaning that I wouldn't fully understand until later. It was time to drive away from the life I had, the life I thought I'd have, and move on to the life I would gain.

We pulled out of the apartment complex I had moved into eleven months prior. My mom had faithfully driven from out of state to move me out as she had done so many times before. In and out of dorm rooms in undergrad. In and out of various places in

60

grad school. This time, she had moved for what I hoped was the last time.

I had relocated for Michael, for the promise of marriage, and like I said, eleven months later, I was moving again because it was over.

As I shed a few more tears and started the seven-hour journey home, I clung to my friend's words. "Don't look back." I didn't. I literally refused to look in the rearview mirror. Truthfully, I was scared to look back. It felt like something spiritual. Perhaps judgment was coming on my ex for being so awful to me. Maybe it was God emancipating me for a brand new life, but I wouldn't see the fruit of it if I kept looking back. I'm not sure. But, I was determined to attain my happy ending even if God has to rewrite the script in heaven just for me.

It was June 2012 and I was back where I had attended grad school. I had just started my new job. I was thrilled to be working again in higher education with a student population. This would be my new start.

That summer was also first time joining a gym at the university where I was newly employed. Although I had a still had few friends in the area from the first time I lived there, we hadn't reconnected at that point. I knew I needed a distraction and I figured exercise could be just that. At the time, Zumba had been very popular for a few years, but I had never tried it. Since I was eager to get back to the things I enjoyed, I knew dance was the perfect place to start.

I'll never forget my first class. About ten of us were standing around waiting for the instructor; then walks in this brown skin girl with raven curls. She wasn't more than 5'4 but I was immediately captivated by this athletic Mona Lisa who carried herself with a kind of self-assurance that said I can teach Zumba or punch you in the face. This girl was as strong as she was beautiful and embodied everything I wanted to be. Maybe this would be more than just a fun workout after all.

Once the pulsating rhythms of the vibrant Latin music started, it was off to the races. It didn't take long for smiles to spread across glistening faces and for even the shyest participant to cut loose. I loved it. I had never moved like that before. I wasn't that great at it at first. In fact, I felt pretty awkward trying to mimic what I saw. I was trained mostly in ballet and modern. I had taken some jazz, African, and hip hop classes. But Latin rhythms were completely new for me.

There was fast footwork and sensual hip action. I felt a little embarrassed at parts, but it was undeniably fun. While a part of me was unacquainted with the new way of moving another part of me took to it easily, as if I had always done it. Moreover, it freed me.

It allowed me to let go in a way that I never have before. I think if I had resumed the ballet and modern styles I was trained in,

I would've been too technically focused and missed the bigger

purpose in moving. Dance isn't always about perfect execution or

proper alignment and technique. It's about freedom, expression,

and connection—and for me, connection to my forgotten self.

Even though I completely fumbled through my first class, I

knew before it was over that I would come back. By the end of

class, I was actually smiling and laughing and it was genuine. I

knew in that moment that Zumba would be pivotal in bringing me

back to life. After that first class with Mona Lisa (I later learned

was Semone), she became my favorite instructor and I became a class regular. Classes were Mondays, Wednesdays, and Fridays at 5:15 that summer, and I went right after work as often as I could. With each class I got a little better. I learned the choreography and got comfortable with the new way of moving my body. It wasn't about perfection or forcing my body to contort in a way that wasn't natural. It was about completely loosing myself and finding myself again.

Yes, I've always been a dancer. I guess it makes sense I'd gravitate toward dance fitness. It felt deeper than that though. But what is the hook exactly? What's so healing about *this* kind of dance? I believe the answer lies in the therapeutic power of dance. It takes connects us to ourselves and to others.

Picture it like this. Imagine those beautiful, indigenous cultures that would come together in the village square. Led by tribal leaders, neighbors would gather together in music and dance. If one person was suffering, then it impacted the entire community. Therefore, the cure was a community event. It's as if dance itself was the conduit for wholeness.[23] Individuals came out of isolation and came into relationship with each other. That's what makes a person whole.

In that sense, Zumba did become so much more than a workout for me. It was more than just a fun dance party. It was more than just a healthy activity to do. It was more than a distraction from a broken heart. It became a vehicle for finding me again and finding a sense of community. Resurrecting my first love of dance was also spiritual experience. It's exactly like Mandy Hale wrote in her book, *Never Been to Vegas*:

> *All the months of grief, sadness, and turmoil were*
> *exorcised on the dance floor, and I held nothing back. And*
> *as I started to empty my heart and emotional reserves of all*
> *the dark times I had been through, I started to make room*
> *for uninhibited, unfettered, and uncontrollable joy. That's*
> *the main thing dance represented to me: joy.*[24]

And that joy was the beginning of finding my strength.

Loved Back to Life

It is the relationship that heals.

– Dr. Irvin Yalom

This is one of my favorite quotations is by Dr. Irvin Yalom, a psychiatrist and specialist in group therapy. In context, he is referring to the therapeutic relationship between counselor and client. Fancy techniques and approaches don't matter nearly as much as a trusting therapeutic relationship. That's what allows people to heal. I take it a step farther and assert that it is any relationship where one feels unconditionally loved and accepted that they start to heal.

I've always valued family and friends. But I didn't realize until the cutoff how isolated I had become in that relationship. You see, as much as I wanted to believe I was living a fairytale, there were dynamics to the relationship, particularly its beginning that I wasn't okay with...namely Michael being in a relationship in the beginning. It's hard for me to even share that...to shamefully admit being the side chick at first.

I'm tempted to offer more details, over-explain, and assure you I'm not a bad person. I want to convince you I had/have morals and I tried to set boundaries throughout the relationship. But, really, there is no defense. The dynamic from the beginning was wrong and it went against my entire value system. All I can really offer is this explanation. *The mind can do all kinds of mental gymnastics to make yourself think you're okay with things you aren't really okay with, especially when you're in love. It can also defend itself against truth that it isn't ready to accept.*

That's why I went in self-protective mode and distanced myself from the people that would tell me the truth because, quite frankly, I didn't want to hear it. I didn't want to be judged. I figured they didn't get it and wouldn't understand that we were meant to be together. I was "The One" and I was legitimate. For a girl who was a surprise pregnancy, whose parents didn't stay

69

together, and whose father didn't stay around, finally feeling legitimate meant everything to me. So, what I did was maintained connections but my life was compartmentalized. It was like I was living two different realities within my love story and it took a toll on me.

Once he left, I slowly but surely started to see clearly again. I saw how I consented to be hidden all those years. I saw that throughout the relationship and even right after I was weird about being on social media because I was afraid. I didn't want to be targeted or outed for the kind of relationship I allowed in my life. Even as I write this book, I desperately don't want to be hated or misunderstood. Shame kept me from wanting to be seen at all. It kept me from putting myself out there at professionally or personally. I carried that shame for years because of the timing of how and when it all started. After getting dumped in that way, I battled thoughts that it was my fault. I should've seen it coming. It was karma. I got what I deserved. I was desperate for support, but also felt like maybe I didn't deserve it.

When I reached out to the people I loved but shut out along the way, I wasn't sure what to expect. I guess on some level I was afraid they would turn me away too. Maybe they would say, "I told you so" or "I saw it all along." I'm not sure why I feared that but it couldn't have been farther from the truth. All of my friends and family surrounded me with warmth and love. Even when they finally got the unedited narrative of the not-so-healthy four-year relationship, I wasn't met with judgment at all- only mercy and grace. That's why to this day one of my favorite verses is, "The one who is forgiven little loves little. The one who is forgiven much loves much" (Luke 7:47). When you experience mercy like that it changes you. You can't help but try to be merciful and compassionate with others.

Friend and family connections were rehabilitative to me during my recovery. There's something powerful about people who have known you a long time coming along and telling you who you are again. Without realizing it I had lost my identity in that relationship. *Despite all my accomplishments, despite being a woman of ambition and standard, I had become all too willing to simply become someone else's wife.* All I wanted was to follow that man to the ends of the earth and I was willing to sacrifice anything, even my soul, to do just that. So, when I lost him I felt as though I lost myself too. It took people loving and affirming me repeatedly to start to dispute the lies he told me in the end.

When I moved back and started my new job the first order of business was to reach out to my girls. It wasn't long before I instituted "group therapy" also known as ladies' night. Usually, it was a night in of food, laughter, and a few bottles of wine. And it was just what I needed. Sometimes we talked about guys or our latest crushes, but mostly it was just enjoying each other. With a couple of acoustic guitar players among us, we were also known to break out in song. We sang everything from the latest contemporary Christian music to the Indigo Girls and No Doubt. It was a blast and that monthly ritual nourished my soul like nothing else.

To this day, my friends mean everything to me. They're my family. I'm no longer afraid to hear the truth from them. I'll tell you this much though. It's much easier to receive a difficult truth about yourself from someone when it's cloaked in love. I might not always like the feedback I receive, but if I'm convinced it's coming from a loving place, I can accept it. My friends are my support system and my cheerleaders. Their opinion carries more weight than that of someone who never knew me or cared to know me. They are the ones who truly see me and love me know matter what. Those relationships healed me and continue to heal me and they brought me back to life.

Strength to Strength

They go from strength to strength until each one appears before

God in Zion.

— Psalm 84:7

I had finally found my rhythm in work and in life. I was

enjoying the work of college counseling. I was still a faithful

regular at Zumba and had even branched out to other group

exercise formats. I had my girls and our regular girls' nights. I

even had a church home again after several years of not going

anywhere. Things had seemed to stabilize and I was, dare I say,

happy. Well, no sooner than I allowed myself to feel secure, I was

rapidly thrust into another huge change. One by one, it seemed all

my single girlfriends defected and got in relationships at the same

time.

I'm not exaggerating. Jennifer was already engaged when I

moved back, so of course, she got married in May. Sarah, who had broken up with her boyfriend that summer, was seeing someone else by August and engaged by Christmas.

Then the biggest surprise was when my quintessential single friend, Jen, who had all but sworn off chances of finding love, met her man in October of that same year. Sarah and Jen were married by the following April. I wanted to be overjoyed for them. Their love stories were well deserved and were a long time coming. Part of me genuinely was. But a bigger part, I'm ashamed to say, was hurt, angry, and heartbroken all over again. By this time, it had been almost two years since the annihilation of my relationship. I had no prospects and now, no friends...or so it felt at the time. I still had them, technically, but they were about to be very different relationships than I had gotten used to, especially with one becoming an army wife and moving overseas.

Needless to say, the girls' nights went from fewer and farther between to non-existent. The dream job in college counseling was becoming a lot less dreamy as I started facing conflicts with co-workers and supervisors. The only positive constant was my time at the university recreation center. But even that had changed since my favorite instructor, Semone, wasn't offering class times that fit my schedule.

Since I knew she was a personal trainer as well and she'd be graduating soon, I decided to hire her. My fitness goals were kind of vague. I mentioned maybe wanting to run my first 5k. I also wanted to get "toned." But really, I just found myself in the position of needing to fill the space again. I needed a friend and something to look forward to. I figured why not hire a workout buddy? And so it began. My first Zumba instructor became my first trainer.

The morning of my first fitness assessment I was scared out of my wits. I'm not sure why exactly. I'd imagine depending how you feel about your body some parts of the assessment would be more anxiety provoking than others. There is a scale involved, not a sensitive area for me, but definitely for many other people. There's a vitals check to measure blood pressure and heart rate. Both were high for me. I guess my anxiety was still up and my physiology was bracing for the next attack.

There's a body composition component that involves a bit of prodding and pinching with a body fat measuring apparatus, enough to make anyone a little insecure. Then that was that. It was time to get started.

We started in January 2014 and met Saturday mornings that entire spring semester. It didn't matter as much now that I didn't have plans anymore on Friday nights. At least I had something to look forward to on Saturdays. Again, I didn't have a real clear goal for having a trainer. I just felt weak and fragile and I desperately wanted to get stronger- internally first, then externally.

So each training session became a therapy session for me.

Every bicep curl, tricep dip, and shoulder raise, every lunge, leg

press, and jump squat taught me to push through and fight. I

remember one time my entire body was trembling while holding a

plank. In the moment, I felt another wave of unprocessed emotion

rise to the surface.

I wanted to cry. I wanted to quit. Instead, I breathed and

pressed through. If anyone tells you they enjoy the sensation of

lifting weights in the moment it's happening, I'd be very

suspicious. Nothing about it feels good at the time. It's the sense of

accomplishment afterwards that gives people the high.

That's what strength training became for me, at least. It was

a way to push myself to the limits and realize I can handle more

than I think I can. More notable than any physical changes I saw,

were the psychological changes that kept me going. I was forced to

start to reframe my view of the shy, scrawny teenager I used to be,

to the woman who grows in strength and confidence each day. As I did that, I decided it was time for yet another challenge. This time

it was running.

> **For physical training is of some value, but spiritual training has value for all things, holding promise for the present life and the life to come."**
>
> **– 1 Timothy 4:8**

Girl on the Run

Therefore, since we are surrounded by such a great cloud of witnesses, let us throw off everything that hinders and the sin that so easily entangles. And let us run with perseverance the race marked out for us.

– Hebrews 12:1

When I mentioned the idea of running my first 5k, it wasn't because I've always been a runner. In fact, it was quite the opposite. In junior high, I always opted to walk the mile instead of run it for time. In eighth grade, my middle school had this horrible idea of having a field day. Hadn't the uncoordinated and athletically awkward suffered through enough of those in elementary school? Unfortunately, they were back that year and since I was forced to choose an event, I chose the sprint. Please don't ask me why. I suppose I reasoned that if I ran quickly it would be over quickly. The entire school looked on from the bleachers as the competitors lined up on the track at the

80

neighboring high school. The signal went off and so did I. I started out strong. I kept pace pretty well until I quickly lost steam and the rest of my peers whizzed by me.

Needless to say, it was a humiliating defeat. It wasn't even a competition. I was completely left in the dust. That's just one of a handful of embarrassing running memories from my past, all contributing to my insistence that I was unequivocally *not* a runner.

Despite my lack of speed and endurance at the time, I seemed to have a lot of runners in my life. Three friends in particular, all named Jennifer, had particularly impressive running records. Between the three of them, these rock star Jennifers have run fifteen half marathons, eight full marathons, and over ten shorter races over the last few years. One particularly hardcore Jen ran the Mega which is pretty much a marathon/hike through the woods of Pennsylvania. I mean, seriously. Who does that? They all seemed to get into it after age 30. If it were solely about physical

81

fitness, I'm sure they would've eventually let it go, just like any other fad workout. Instead, something about running moved them figuratively and literally. When I explored it with them, this is what I learned. Running appealed to them socially, physically, emotionally, and spiritually.

Socially

Each of them started because of a friend's encouragement. One said, "After some conversation with friends where I said I could NEVER run a half marathon, they signed me up for it anyway…I got bit by the running bug and have been running ever since." Someone in their life made them feel like they could, so they did. Then once they started, they became part of a community.

Not only do their loved ones cheer them on at races, but so do complete strangers. There's nothing like a crowd of people you don't even know cheering you on and telling you that you can do it.

Physically

There are lots of benefits to aerobic activity. It helps with weight management, prevents a sedentary lifestyle, and keeps the body regulated. One shared proudly, "My doctor has told me that since running my cholesterol looks good. My blood pressure is, and I quote her, "beautiful." These Jennifers seemed to eat better, sleep better, and feel better when they ran. And given the physical toll my body had taken after the breakup, I figured I needed something rigorous to discharge all that negative energy and recalibrate my whole system.

Emotionally

Each one mentioned running as a form of stress relief. It offered a solace to process the issues of life. One shared how healing it is for her. "When I was going through a painful time in my life, the marathon training helped me process my emotions and feelings by replaying what had happened until it stopped hurting so badly." Running was her therapy.

Spiritually

Lastly, running was about nurturing their spirits. "It gets me outdoors enjoying God's creation, and gives me time and space to clear my head and just get with God." Through that consecrated time of prayer and meditation they learned these key life lessons: a) Keep moving, b) Be patient with yourself, c) Do it for you, d) Embrace all seasons, and e) You can do anything you set your mind to.

I have tremendous respect for the Jennifers in my life. I've heard their stories. I've witnessed their setbacks and triumphs. I'm blessed to be running life's marathon with them. Because of them, I was inspired to try running as well. That's when I decided to sign up for my first 5k.

As I was conditioning for my first race, Semone asked me what the hardest thing about running was. I told her that it wasn't so much fatigue in my legs and muscles. For me, running is just the most intense exercise I can do. I'm pretty sure I was close to my maximum heart rate because my heart always felt like it was going to beat out of my chest. I wasn't out of shape at that point either. I had been working out consistently for almost two years. But running was by far, was the most physiologically rigorous activity I had ever tried.

In one of my personal training sessions, we were running a couple of miles to prep for the 5k. I was trying to play it cool because she made it look so easy. But I was panting like crazy and trying not to collapse. At some point though, after she had gotten a few paces ahead, I slowed down to a walk. In a gentle, yet firm way, like any good coach would do, she urged me to keep going and try not to slow down. Somehow, I made it back to our starting point without fainting or getting sick, thank you very much. Then, she was gracious enough to let me catch my breath and hydrate before starting sprinting exercises.

And it was the same process... I wanted to be done and then I was gently, yet firmly challenged to go "one more time." By the way, any trainer who tells you "one more time" is lying. They really mean three to five more times. It's just what I needed though. If left alone, I would've stopped. With a supportive guide there I did more than I thought I could. I think that's what people mean when they say exercise is all mental. If I couldn't physically handle it, my body would've given out. But by simply believing I could keep going, that's apparently all I needed to keep pushing.

It's a lot like a term in fitness called overloading. Essentially, what it means is that in order to improve, the body system must be stressed beyond its normal level and it will adapt.

The mind and body are indivisibly connected. If you tell yourself you can't, then you can't. If you tell yourself you can, you can. It's that simple. Then your physiology catches up with whatever internal truth you accept. It's pretty amazing.

There's also a lot to be said about just continuing to put one foot in front of the other. It's not particularly novel but it is profound. While running your course, sometimes it helps to disregard the finish line. Sometimes seeing it can make the final steps the hardest ones to take. Just focus on the step in front of you. I'm a smart girl. I had a hunch Semone was trying to pull one over with the whole "one more time" line. Yet and still, I shifted mentally and ran with my all when I told myself it was my last time. I drew upon energy I didn't know was there. Such is life…keep running your race, one foot diligently in front of the other, challenging yourself to go farther than you ever thought you could, and you'll be amazed when you reach the finish line. It doesn't matter how you stumbled or struggled on your way there. It's about persevering.

That perseverance helped me successfully complete my first 5k and five other subsequent races and counting. Each training period held new revelations and each race was different from the previous. Each training period had its own story and its own theme. Sometimes I ran with friends and enjoyed the victory with others. Other times, I ran alone and learned the power of encouraging myself.

One of many lessons I've gained from running is this: if I ever have to go at something alone, I can do it. It's not necessarily my preference and it's not always necessary for each season of life. But if ever it's called for me to run my race solo, I can do it because I have what it takes to endure.

Breathe Again

And breathe, just breathe. Oh breathe, just breathe.

– Anne Nalick, "Breathe (2AM)"[25]

The first 5k race sealed the deal for me. Fitness was officially a lifestyle and I had no plans of turning back. It was so much a part of me now that I even got licensed to teach Zumba, certified in group exercise, and eventually became a personal trainer. It's fascinating because no one told me to start working out. I just seemed to intuitively know that exercise could be my very own and no one could take it from me. What started as simple walking and regular attendance to Zumba class, soon spread to strength training and then running. I had always known there were health benefits to exercise as they have been well documented. It's great for stress relief with all the endorphins released and such. But as I keep saying, it was more than that. Movement served to rehabilitate me and I was curious why.

90

Dr. Peter Levine, author of *Waking the Tiger: Healing Trauma*, describes it this way:

> *Traumatic symptoms are not caused by the "triggering" event itself. They stem from the frozen residue of energy that has not been resolved and discharged; this residue remains trapped in the nervous system where it can wreak havoc in our bodies and spirits. The long-term, alarming, debilitating, and often bizarre symptoms of PTSD develop when we cannot complete the process of moving in, through and out of "immobility" or "freezing" state. However, we can thaw by initiating and encouraging our innate drive to return to a state of equilibrium.*[26]

For me, it makes sense, then, that if a person experiences any sort of physical, mental, or emotional trauma, even the little "t" traumas of normal life, then the healing should occur in the soul and the body. When people experience any level of threat, the brain fires off and stress hormones are released. The function is to

91

move us to action once the fight or flight mechanism is activated in our brains. I've heard it explained this way. If you think you can beat your enemy, you'll fight. If you think you can outrun your enemy, you'll flee. If you can't do either, you'll freeze and play dead.

All of these are valid responses and serve as survival mechanisms to cope with the threat until it passes. The women I interviewed and I, we were initially immobilized, or frozen, by the loss. It's hard to even breathe, more or less, to move when you're in shock. When you consider the trauma of betrayal by a loved one, it's easy to see why.

> "How do I live without you? I want to know; how do I breathe without you? If you ever go…"
>
> – Leann Rimmes, "How Do I Live"

Attachment theories describe how we are as emotionally dependent on our partner as a child is on his or her caregiver.[27] So, when your person suddenly disconnects, the jilted party is left vulnerable. At times, there is no way to prepare emotionally or psychologically for the departure and that leaves the one who is left with trapped energy that needs to be discharged.

Although I didn't expect to find this, I learned that all the women in my interviews used some form of exercise as a coping resource after their breakups:

I run a lot—training for a marathon.

Yoga, swimming, running...

(Exercise) became a saving grace for me emotionally.

This could be due to the outlet it affords to discharge the intense emotion on a physical level. It could also be because the breakup inspired an appropriate self-focus (Sakraida) in which we now had the freedom to focus on our needs.

That's exactly what I needed next. I had found great outlets to release the pain. Now, I needed an outlet to restore the balance. That's when I returned to my yoga practice after a few years away from it. I figured yoga would afford me a contemplative space that

I very much needed during a time of transition. Once again, at the university recreation center, I found another favorite instructor, Jocelyn, to guide me on a new journey.

Jocelyn was a fiery redhead and Navy veteran. I liked her because she wasn't your typical yoga instructor that spoke in soft tones and always seemed to be communing with nature. In fact, one time she entered her 6am class ranting about how bad traffic was. Before we got a good morning, I remember her walking in briskly and saying, "Traffic makes me the angriest."

I appreciated her realness, especially that early in the morning. That morning rant really endeared her to me that day and I knew I was going to like her. At any rate, here are some simple lessons I learned from her yoga classes.

Be Intentional

At the beginning of each practice we were invited to set an intention. It could be a prayer or positive vibe to someone in need. It could be love or a positive affirmation for ourselves. It could also just be to remain mindfully present on the mat for the duration of practice.

I could always tell a difference when I just went through the motions versus being intentional about what I hoped to gain from my practice. If you're too open and want to receive everything, you probably won't get anything, so fix your gaze on your true desire.

Focus Determines Direction

Each week we spent some time on a balancing pose. Crow pose is essentially holding your entire body weight in your arms. You definitely need upper body strength but it's also about correct positioning and alignment. A tip Jocelyn gave was to look slightly ahead of you without looking too far ahead because your body will go where your eyes go. That was significant to me as I learned to let go of the past and look ahead toward my future.

Breathe through Difficulty

One thing I love about exercise but especially yoga is that it reminds you to breathe. Generally, the first thing we do in stress or distress is hold our breath. Exercise puts your body under physiological stress. Yoga conditions you to keep breathing in spite of that stress. Eventually, the discomfort passes and you learn to tolerate distress while you gain strength.

Find Your Stability

Again, with balancing poses, most people want to immediately go to the full expression of the pose. But if your foundation is weak, you won't have the strength or balance to achieve the pose or maintain it if you get there. So, it's essential to get grounded where you are and once you are secure challenge yourself to go further.

Honor Where You Are Today

The final lesson from yoga practice is the importance of accepting yourself right where you are. Human beings are so dynamic that we not only change day by day but moment by moment as well. That's why each new expression of a pose is an invitation to go deeper. Some days you can and other days you cannot. It takes discipline to remove the "shoulds" from your mindset and accept reality for what it is today. You are where you are today and you'll get to where you're going tomorrow with intention, focus, endurance, stability, and radical self-acceptance.

That's the cool thing about yoga for me. It's as much about the philosophy as it is the practice itself. It's a discipline that encourages introspection, not just when you're on the mat, but throughout the day.

If you just workout, then you'll get physically fit but that's about it. But if you move mindfully, purposefully including all parts of yourself in the process, then you'll not only condition your body, but you'll condition your spirit and soul too.

Soul Work

May you prosper and be in good health even as your soul prospers

and gets along well.

– 3 John 1:2

Movement is healing. There's no doubt about it. It frees you like nothing else. I want to be clear though. Exercise alone didn't heal my broken heart. It helped reduce my sadness and anxiety. It gave me a positive outlet to release grief and anger. At some point though, I had to address my soul.

My personal and professional tag line is Bible verse, 3 John 1:2, "May you prosper and be in good health even as your soul prospers." I love this. What it means to me is that you can only be as well on the outside as you are on the inside. There are plenty of people in peak physical condition that are an emotional wreck. They still harbor anger and unforgiveness. They still numb and escape through sex, drugs, or other vices. They still have distorted self-concepts and perhaps even an obsessive relationship to food and exercise.

To me, that's missing the point entirely. You want all aspects of your being to exist in harmony. True wellness requires tending the needs of the body and soul.

The thought occurred to me that there aren't many places for people to reflect on their soul. Unless you've been to therapy or rehab, unless you ascribe to some spiritual or mindfulness tradition, unless you're just naturally inclined to read psychology and self-help books, then you're probably not going to do much soul work, or even consider the need to do so.

Even the language, "do your work" is something completely foreign to many. The work that healers and spiritual teachers speak of is the painful process of inner reflection. It's about taking a fearless personal inventory, facing your demons, identifying and yes, even embracing the dark shadow sides of your personhood. It's about acknowledging all that's happened, even

101

what wrongly happened to you, and allowing it to be part of the beautiful tapestry of a redeemed life.

This work is about "taking the bitter and the sweet of life," as Kim Clement, a Christian teacher says, even the things that people intended for your harm, even that which never should've happened, and seeing how it can be used for your good. As you might imagine though, this work is not easy. It's painful and often avoided.

Yet, this work is instrumental in your becoming. Becoming what? Becoming all that you are destined to be.

During that difficult winter and spring of the breakup, I went back to therapy for the first time in years. I've actually been to counseling several times throughout my life. I'm thankful to have a mom who normalized it for me and always encouraged me to "nip things in the bud" by getting support sooner than later. So, when I received what felt like the blow of my life, I didn't hesitate to find a counselor and start putting the pieces back together.

For about five months, I worked with a wonderful woman named Colby, a psychologist in the area I moved to for Michael. I knew from the initial phone consult that she got me and I was safe to share everything. We met every two weeks and sometimes weekly until I was able to relocate. It's interesting when you work as a counselor and simultaneously receive counseling. I had a wonderfully flexible job at the time, so I would take an extended lunch between my client sessions. Between caring for others and holding their emotions, I would go to Colby and let her hold mine. I poured my heart out to this compassionate stranger as she did psychological first aid on my soul.

For those of you who have never been to counseling, allow me to demystify the process for you. Basically, it's a conversation. You share your thoughts and feelings and any places you feel stuck, and the therapist, in turn, facilitates the process of you getting unstuck. It's not about advice. It's not solely about learning coping strategies. It's really about looking in a mirror and having someone else reflect back your experience. It's hard to describe, but that simple process of someone reflecting what they hear, normalizing it, and validating your emotions- that's the cure. That's the healing balm for a hurting soul.

Once I felt seen and heard, once I knew she understood how awful my ex's actions were and how much they crushed me, I was then able to own my part in it all. No, what happened wasn't my fault. I didn't deserve it, by any means. But counseling showed me how much I idealized Michael and our relationship because of my own unresolved issues. My therapist never said that. I came to see that myself. I was most definitely grieving the relationship loss itself. But there were so many more layers to it...layers of grief that I'd have to learn to let go.

Letting Go

Letting go is hard, but sometimes holding on is harder.

On letting go…I kind of see it like this. You know those Zen-like people who seem blissfully unbothered in life? It's not a feigned indifference. They are genuinely grounded and centered. It's as if truly nothing fazes them. They are probably the ones that can stay friends with their exes. They love with an open heart and give life their all. Then when it's time to let go and move on they do so with willingness and gratitude. I'm so *not* one of those people.

It's sad to say, but I've always been a bit more like Elmyra from *Tiny Toons Adventures* in my relationships. Remember her? She was the little girl who loved animals so much and all she wanted was a pet. She was the one that would say, "I'm going to love you and hold you and squeeze you."

106

She meant well, but she would often come on too strong and nearly smother the poor critter. Can anyone else relate? Do you ever want someone so badly that you ruin it by holding on too tight? Have you unwittingly delved into obsessive, stalker-ish territory by not moving on when it's time? If so, it might help to consider a few things I've learned about holding on and letting go.

There are Layers to Loss

When people lose anything significant in their life, especially relationships, it's rarely just about one loss. There are layers of loss because that person has come to represent so much. For instance, a partner can become your identity and your ideal self. If you date someone you perceive as better than you, then it validates who you are. You automatically become better. They also represent your happily ever after.

You can imagine how difficult it is to let go once your sense of self becomes intertwined in something that might not last.

It's no wonder people kick and scream to hold on even when it's time to let go. In a symbolic sense, their very being depends on it.

You Don't Cling to What's Already Yours

Think about this though. When something truly belongs to you there's no need to fight for it. There's a sense of security and peace because you know it's yours.

When I go to work I have my designated office space. I don't speed to get there early to make sure no one occupies it before I arrive. It's mine. It's the same way with walking to the parking lot at the end of the day. I don't expect anyone to drive off with my car because it's mine. Provided I keep paying the car note and don't park in a tow zone my car should be there each and every time I leave work. Why? Because it's mine. *When you clamor and cleave to force someone to stay, could that signal that you don't really feel secure and maybe you never really did?* It seems the only time we cling desperately is when we fear we might lose it forever.

There's Peace in Release

A final point to consider is how emotionally exhausting it is to keep holding on when it's time to let go. You feel anxious and worried about the object of your desire slipping through your fingers. You lose a bit of dignity when you place an Elmyra-style grip on a relationship and then require Jaws of Life to pry it away. Then you have to deal with the pain of a dramatic severing when it all could've been avoided by knowing when to call it quits.

What if you cared for someone and left room for the relationship to change at any moment? What if you cherished the things in your life and willingly returned them if asked? What if you immediately offered everything in your life back to God recognizing He gave it all in the first place? I just wonder if it's possible to be like those peaceful, Zen-like people by learning to hold on with open hands.

I was able to put this idea in action at my last birthday gathering. Several friends and I went to an outdoor adventure park with ropes courses and ziplining. While the overall park experience was a lot of fun, I can't say that every moment was fun.

There was one particular course where we had to skateboard on a zipline through the trees. You were harnessed in, of course, but that offered no real comfort when all you had to grab onto was the rope overhead.

I didn't love it. I wanted it to be over. That's kind of how life is sometimes. Some experiences just have to be endured until you get to the next moment.

Then there was the letting go part, which I've already shared is really hard for me. Interestingly enough, what I noticed in the trees was that every obstacle that required holding on was much more difficult for me. I was desperately clinging and afraid to fall. I was much more anxious and it was a struggle to balance. It was just harder all around. But each time I could just zipline or let go and ride, it was the most fun I had. There's surprising freedom in just letting go.

Finally, the grand finale of most of the courses was a trust fall. All you had to do was step off a platform of variable heights and land safely on the ground. Oh yeah, and there was no safety exit. Stepping off is the only way down. So it is with life. *When all your back-up plans and emergency exits and maneuvers to self-protect are eliminated, all you can do is step forward and trust.*

Anytime there's change we have to let go. Anytime there's loss we have to let go. Anytime we want to embrace something in the future we have to let go. Letting go is an essential part of transforming into who you were always meant to be.

Overcomer

I wanted you bad. I'm so through with that. 'Cause honestly you

turned out to be the best thing I never had.

– Beyoncé, "Best Thing I Never Had"[28]

When I first made the call to interview women on

breakups, I suppose I just really wanted to hear other women's

stories to know I wasn't alone. Other than that though, I didn't

have any expectations for what I'd find. That's the beauty of

research. You take a sample of individuals who don't know each

other, all of varying ages and ethnic backgrounds, people who

don't have anything else in common except whatever phenomenon

you want to explore. Then, when you somehow find themes in

common, it's almost magical. Perhaps you've caught a glimpse

into the universal human experience.

One of the common themes I found among the interviews

was transformation through loss. Women grew personally and

spiritually after relational loss. Regardless if they were the dumped

112

or the dumper, all of the women in this sample reported a rediscovery of their worth.

> *I learned to be more attentive to myself and really take care of myself...I will always miss him, but I had to let go in order to be where I want to be.*

> *I could never have stayed in that relationship and reached my full potential. I let my relationship come before myself and my health, and I never want that to happen again.*

> *I believe I am stronger and smarter in terms of facing those unexpected, traumatic changes in life.*

Not only did the women feel empowered in themselves, but they also believed that the experience of the loss made them better people.

> **"It should kill you...but it doesn't. Instead it leaves you wounded. Flattened. Broken. But alive. It should kill you...but it doesn't. Instead, it leaves you stronger."**
>
> **– Mandy Hale, *Beautiful Uncertainty***

I turned my thinking from "this is a horrible experience" to "this is a chance for growth in myself".

No one can ever take everything away from you if you are holding all your pieces together yourself. It took me hitting rock bottom for me to start over and rebuild myself as a new, stronger person. I realized that in order for me to ever have hope of being happy with anyone else I had to be happy by/with myself first.

I learned that I am so much stronger than I ever thought I was. I also learned that anyone can turn their lives around and work toward happiness no matter what they have been through. This loss does not rule my life.

[29] I was in tears as I listened to the recordings of the interviews and transcribed these statements over and over. They mirrored exactly what I felt—from the initial blow to the empowered recovery process. Every one of these statements demonstrates the power of resilience. We could have been

permanently scarred by the loss and immobilized by the experience. Instead, we took the challenge as an opportunity, an obstacle to overcome and an experience from which to learn.

That is not to say these women or I are no longer hurt by the event. On the contrary, many expressed that they still cry over the loss, they still care deeply for their former partner, and they have difficulty trusting and being open in new relationships. What we all agree on, however, is that there is life after loss and if this pain has brought us to a greater sense of self-knowledge, then it is or will be worth it in the long run.

It's easy to blame the people in your life for your personal misery: jerk exes, critical or deadbeat parents, fake friends, lousy bosses, jealous colleagues, etc. But when you make it all about them you remain a victim. You see life as a series of things that have wrongly happened to you and you forfeit your power. When you shift your view and see how every challenge was designed to strengthen you, then you step up to the plate. You step up and decide that you will be great *in spite of* what happened. This is

what it takes to be an overcomer.

Athlete of God

I believe that we learn by practice. Whether it means to learn to dance by practicing dancing or to learn to live by practicing living, the principles are the same...One becomes, in some area, an athlete of God.

– Martha Graham[30]

If you told me a few years ago, that I would be a runner, weight lifter, and personal trainer, I would've laughed in your face. I liked moving, especially dance, but I was definitely no athlete. Yet, here I am with an entirely new identity that I never thought possible. It was in losing what I thought was everything that I gained my true life—the one I was always meant to live.

As I said in the beginning, I share all of this because it's my story, my experience. The relationship loss changed my life completely. It brought me back to where I started. It serendipitously brought me fitness. It brought me to my knees in

118

the rawest prayer and worship you can imagine. It required me to stand strong even though a part of me wanted to curl up and die.

Most of all, it unleashed my warrior inside. I never would have known my own resilience unless I had something to bounce back from. No one wants to sign up for suffering. We're creatures of comfort and generally avoid harm. There is good that can come from adversity though if you allow it to make you and not break you.

I believe all of us will have to face something in this life. For some, it's cancer or some other health crisis. For others, it's losing a child or parent, someone we never thought we could live without. Maybe it's financial devastation or job loss.

Maybe it's overcoming a painful childhood trauma. Everyone's transformative life experience is different, but there will be something. It's almost as if there's an opposing force out there who wants to keep you from being all you were created to be. It's as if the trial was uniquely designed to destroy you. But God…By the grace of God, you'll face that challenge and say, *Do no gloat over me, my enemy. Though I fall, I will rise. Though I sit in darkness the Lord will be my light* (Micah 7:8). You might feel broken at first and down for the count. Then something within you will stand up. Your grief will turn into determination and will move you forward. Through the tears and anguish you will keep moving and learn there is life after loss.

So, here I am today as a new creation. I'm a mover, a warrior, an athlete of God. Every movement style I engage in gives me a new metaphor for healing and overcoming in life. Every physical challenge is met with a mental challenge as I continually learn that I'm stronger than I think I am.

Whenever I think about my biggest battle to date and how it all went down, I'm reminded of and echo the sentiments of one woman I interviewed:

It was a hit. It was a hard hit. But it didn't knock me down.

Epilogue

And if I'm flying solo, at least I'm flying free...

– from *Wicked*[31]

Because you're probably wondering what happened with me in the love department, I feel obliged to share. Still no man. Not yet at least. That's a part of the story that's still awaiting redemption. I would like to think that makes me a more honest, relatable character though. Because, be honest. If I said that after all that awfulness, I met and married an amazing man a year later, wouldn't some of you have rolled your eyes and tossed the book across the room? Or closed out your browser? Maybe you'd think I didn't really get it because I had crossed over into happily partnered bliss. Perhaps you'd view me as out of touch. Well, I'm not. And because I'm not, I think I owe you one more honest chapter on the productive and non-productive ways I've managed singleness.

Productive Ways

Not Dating

After a breakup like that, it takes time to really heal. This wasn't the sort of thing you bounce back from in a few weeks or even months. For me, it ended up taking a couple of years before I was open to opening my heart again. Admittedly, there's no set timeline and it doesn't always take that long for everyone. There are always exceptions to the rule. I do think it's safe to say that need more than five seconds to recover though. However, some people do opt to dive back in immediately. While sometimes it works out for the best and that's their unique story, I think for a lot of people, it just doesn't work in the long run. Often, you're simply distracting yourself from the pain. And for those that do get a new boo, bae, beau, what have you, right away, I can't help but think you're doing yourself a disservice. You don't have to face the childhood wounds that the breakup triggered. You can ignore your role in it. You don't have to tolerate the spiritual open heart surgery required after feeling so completely unloved. You can push all of that aside and feel the reverie of being attached to someone. I'm sorry to say but that's a cop out. It's much harder to journey solo for a while and let healing take place. It's much harder to place a Do Not Disturb sign on your heart for a while, as Pastor Kim Pothier ("Real Talk Kim") says. It hasn't been easy, but I am thankful I've chosen that path.

Pursuing Purpose

Another productive way I've spent my singleness is by focusing on what I'm meant to do. In a way, the whole breakup ordeal set me on a totally new career trajectory. I discovered that I'm an athlete and now fitness a huge part of my personal and professional life.

Not only that, but in my season of singleness, I've started my own wellness business and completed several projects that I think will help people. Namely, this book. I doubt I would've had the urgency to finish it up if I were up under somebody all the time. So, you know...you're welcome. ☺ But seriously, there's a real principle in scripture about the single person having undivided devotion to the Lord. She/he is only concerned with the things of God. Therefore, I'm honored to do my Father's business with minimal distractions.

Learning from Others

What's also been a good use of singleness, as well as an unexpected gift, is learning from the relationships of those around me. I watch the friends that get it right and those that don't. I see

the turmoil of many clients struggling through relationship

concerns. I see how even okay marriages can erode over time and

how bad relationships become even more toxic with time. While I

hate to see others' suffering, I'm thankful for having a window into

their life. It's like God is showing me the future I would've had

with Michael had He not intervened. For that, I'm truly thankful.

Unproductive Ways

Not Dating

Now, for the unproductive ways I've managed being

alone...and yes, I'm well aware that "Not dating" is on this list too.

But, it's appropriately and intentionally on both lists. There's

something to be said about taking an adequate amount of time to

grieve. It's very subjective and variable and only you really know

how long that is.

There's also something to be said about easing back in and

not avoiding. Avoidance only reinforces fear. And if I'm honest,

126

guys have become big, scary monsters to me simply because I've avoided interacting with them for so long. That's not healthy and I'm working on overcoming that. How do you know if God isn't orchestrating a new relational experience to emotionally correct the previous, if you stay holed up in your self-protective shell? Again, don't jump in too soon, but at some point, be willing to dip your toe in.

Baes in my Head

Another unproductive way I've coped with singleness is by creating baes in my head. For those who are new to the term, bae, it's pretty much just a derivative of baby and a term of endearment…kind of like boo was in the '90s and early 2000s.

At any rate, this is a term I made up based off the MTV *Girl Code* segment, "My best friend in my head." In the segment, the hosts talk about someone famous and why he or she is "my best friend in my head." I honestly thought I was alone in the silly tendency to form an attachment to someone who has no idea.

While it might be harmless enough, although no less stalker-ish, to form a friendship crush, it can be emotionally dangerous to create a bae in your head. Yet, over the years, I've done this more times than I care to admit. It's as if a real connection with someone is too threatening. But if I can pine for them from afar, then I get all the same energy and excitement of a crush, without the fear of rejection. Makes sense, right? Well, it does until it back fires.

The thing with unrequited infatuation (notice I didn't say love) is that it's brutal. It's not romantic at all to have a one-sided affair. And the danger is that even though the person doesn't belong to you, it kind of feels like they do. You have all the same jealousy and possessiveness as if you were in an actual relationship with them, except they have no idea and certainly aren't responsible for how you feel.

So, when you learn your bae is with someone else, it sends you over the edge for a while. It's embarrassing to admit, but this is a way that I've coped with loneliness, if I'm perfectly honest. I've fallen for people who don't belong to me. See a theme here? And when I realize I can't have them and never will, it triggers deep pain and grief all over again.

It's emotionally exhausting and unproductive. It's also not fair to the poor person who has no clue and it's not fair to you. The best bet is to guard your heart so you don't set up false expectations and get disappointed.

Hating

I know it's incredibly petty of me to admit, but a third unproductive way I've dealt with singleness is by internally hating on the couples of the world. I have to be honest. While it definitely isn't all the time and it's not a reaction I have across the board, sometimes on my bad days seeing engagement, wedding, and anniversary posts, date night pics and Man Crush Monday shout

outs, send my eyes all the way to the back of my head.

It frustrates me when love happens so easily for others and

it's been such a struggle for me. I have watched more people than I

can count breakup with someone and get with somebody else just a

few months later. They don't appear to be rebound scenarios

necessarily. It's just in the course of living their lives they're

fortunate enough to meet someone new. It just doesn't take them

long. As I said, that's *never* been my story.

But, here's the thing. It's not about denying others their

happy ending. It was never that when my friends met their

husbands either. It was just dealing with the bigger feeling of when

will I get mine? Why am I being left out of such an important

milestone? Why is it so hard for me meet a decent guy and make a

go at forever? Is something wrong with me? Am I invisible?

Not long ago, I feel like I got my answer. I went to hear my

friend, Gary, speak at his church and the message was "What is

God hiding and why?" Talk about timely. He had a few points related to how and why God conceals some things and readily reveals others.

The point that hit home for me related to God hiding people. Basically, God will often hide people for their own protection. He shared, "God will make you invisible for the sake of your calling. He's placed unique things inside of you. He will protect you from unhealthy influences because he knows relational decisions will have a generational effect."

Furthermore, he explained that sometimes we're hidden so we don't get in our own way or ruin what God has for us. "Only He knows what you look like when your dreams come true." To me, that's pretty powerful. I'm not hidden because I'm worthless. I'm hidden because I'm special and God wants to lovingly safeguard what's meant for me. That's not just a lesson for singles. That's for all of us.

It reminds me of a conference I went to about twelve years ago. I heard motivational speaker, Lynette Lewis. At the time, she was Lynette Troyer. She shared very openly about being forty and never married. She had a successful career in New York City. She was active in ministry. She was and still is a very attractive and gifted woman and yet for a good part of her adult life her biggest desire for marriage and family went unfulfilled. But even in sharing her story through tears, she wasn't at all bitter or desperate and she possessed no ounce of self-pity. In fact, I remember her very intentionally universalizing her experience to all of us. She said that we're all waiting for something. Whether it's a life mate, a family, a home, a new job opportunity, a shot at making it big, we're all waiting for something. It goes back to the process, the soul work. Everyone's life experience is different. Their struggle, their challenge. But there will be something that perfectly brings to surface everything that God wants to heal. Apparently, God sees the best learning environment for me is in my singleness…at least for right now.

On singleness…it ain't easy. It takes a lot of courage to fly solo in a couples' world. For some people, it's enormously freeing and they feel empowered to live life on their own terms. For those who long for love, however, it's okay to struggle with it. Just recognize that there's beauty in the longing. There's beauty in the tension. There's beauty in the in between. That's the part that makes you human and connects you with God, if you have the courage to take it to Him. It's hard, but I urge you to yield that vulnerable side to Him. Yield that longing for companionship, affection, intimate touch…yield that desire to belong to someone and be covered…yield that desire to be seen as valuable and lovable by others. That's right. It's not just about getting your person. It's about showing him/her off to the world too, so be real about that.

He'll not only respond to the deepest desires and secret petitions of your heart. *He'll do two very important things that are even better than getting your answered prayer: 1) He'll give you the grace to find satisfaction in the gift and 2) He'll remove the sting of shame for ever having gone so long without it.* That's what I believe, at least.

Acknowledgments

I want to give a huge thanks to my editing team and wonderful friends, Jennifer Scott and Sarah Nguyen. You guys not only restored me through our girls' nights. You took my story in its raw form and helped me shape it into a piece that makes me proud. I couldn't have done it without you.

I want to thank my dear friend, Jenn Del Corso. You walked the closest with me through the darkest time of my life. You held my heart and reminded me to breathe. Without your emails, texts, and phone calls several times a day during those months, I really don't know where I would be. I'm so glad God sent me you during that time. Feel free to bill me.

A big thank you to my photographer friends, Andrew Jatau and Michael Clay. You captured the joy and strength of my journey and I'm grateful.

I want to thank my mom, my sister, and all of my wonderful friends, whom I am blessed to say are too numerous to

136

name. Each one of you loved me back to life. Thank you for praying and warring for me when I was too weak to fight for myself.

And to all of my fitness friends, thank you for taking me in and letting me hang with the cool kids. You guys are my fitspiration. I will always have fond memories of you because I met you in what became my happy place. I'm not sure I would've chosen the path that led me to you, but I am eternally thankful for the outcome. Much love.

About the Author

Dr. Crista Gambrell is a passionate woman committed to actively pursuing a joy-filled, vibrant life, and helping others do the same. She is a licensed professional counselor in Coastal Virginia and has been practicing for the last ten years. She specializes in women's issues, including but not limited to balance and self-care, exercise and eating concerns, and healthy relationships. She particularly enjoys working with college age and young adult women navigating normal life issues.

Crista is also a certified personal training and a certified wellness coach. She teaches Zumba and other group exercise formats as well as trains clients individually. When she is not working she cherishes time with family and friends, exploring new places, and writing. To learn

more, please visit www.gambrellwellness.com.

End Notes

[1] Susan Sprecher, Corinne Zimmerman, & Erin M. Abrahams, "Choosing Compassionate Strategies to End a Relationship: Effects of Compassionate Love for Partner and the Reason for the Breakup," *Social Psychology* 41, no. 2 (2010): 66-75.

[2] Ibid.

[3] Jordan S. Robinson & Christine Larson, "Are Traumatic Events Necessary to Elicit Symptoms of Posttraumatic Stress?," *Psychological Trauma: Theory, Research, Practice, and Policy* 2, no. 2 (2010): 71-76.

[4] Toni Braxton, "Un-Break My Heart," in *Secrets*, LaFace, 1996, MP3.

[5] *Sex and the City*, "Ex and the City," HBO, October 3, 1999, written by Michael Patrick King.

[6] Elizabeth Gilbert, Twitter Post, May 6, 2015, 4:20pm, https://twitter.com/gilbertliz.

[7] Jordin Sparks and Chris Brown, "No Air," in *Jordin Sparks*, Jive, 2007, MP3

[8] *Sex and the City*, "The Post-It Always Sticks Twice," HBO, August 3, 2003, written by Liz Tuccillo.

[9] Ibid.

[10] Susan Sprecher, Corinne Zimmerman, & Erin M. Abrahams, "Choosing Compassionate Strategies to End a Relationship: Effects of Compassionate Love for Partner and the Reason for the Breakup," *Social Psychology* 41, no. 2 (2010): 66-75.

[11] Ibid.

[12] Duncan Sheik, "Barely Breathing," in *Duncan Sheik*, Atlantic Records, 1996, MP3.

[13] Kem, "Why Would You Stay," in *Intimacy: Album II*, Universal Motown, 2010, MP3.

[14] Adele, "Set Fire to the Rain," in *21*, Columbia, 2011, MP3.

[15] Jordan S. Robinson & Christine Larson, "Are Traumatic Events Necessary to Elicit Symptoms of Posttraumatic Stress?," *Psychological Trauma: Theory, Research, Practice, and Policy* 2, no. 2 (2010): 71-76; Christian J. Dean, "Psychoeducation: The First Step to Understanding Infidelity-Related Systemic Trauma and Grieving," *The Family Journal* 19, no. 1 (2010): 15-21.

[16] Christian J. Dean, "Psychoeducation: The First Step to Understanding Infidelity-Related Systemic Trauma and Grieving," *The Family Journal* 19, no. 1 (2010): 15-21.

[17] Warren H. Jones, Danny S. Moore, Arianne Schratter, & Laura A. Negel, "Interpersonal Transgressions and Betrayals," in *Behaving Badly: Aversive Behaviors in Interpersonal Relationships*, ed. Robin M. Kowalski (Washington, DC: American Psychological Association, 2001), 237.

[18] Adele, "Rolling in the Deep," in *21*, Columbia, 2011, MP3.

[19] Donald Lawrence and the Tri-City Singers, "Seasons," in *Go Get Your Life Back*, EMI Gospel, 2002, MP3.

[20] Marvin Sapp, "He Has His Hands on You," in *Here I Am*, Verity Records, 2010, MP3.

[21] Dwight David, "The Last Dragon," in *The Last Dragon*, Motown Records, 1985, MP3.

[22] Gotye, "Somebody That I Used to Know," in *Making Mirrors*, Eleven: A Music Company, 2011, MP3.

[23] Ilene Serlin, "Root Images of Healing in Dance Therapy," *American Journal of Dance Therapy* 15, no. 2 (1993): 65-76.

[24] Mandy Hale, *I've Never Been to Vegas but My Luggage Has: Mishaps and Miracles on the Road to Happily Ever After* (Nashville, TN: Nelson Books, 2014), 91.

[25] Anna Nalick, "Breathe (2am)," in *Wreck of the Day*, Columbia, 2005, MP3.

[26] Peter A. Levine, *Waking the Tiger: Healing Trauma* (Berkeley, CA: North Atlantic Books, 1997), 19-20.

[27] Harville Hendrix, *Getting the Love You Want: A Guide for Couples, 20th Anniversary Edition* (New York, NY: Holt Paperbacks, 2008); Sue Johnson, *Hold Me Tight: Seven Conversations for a Lifetime of Love* (New York, NY: Little, Brown and Company, 2008).

[28] Beyoncé, "Best Thing I Never Had," in *4*, Columbia, 2011, MP3.

[29] Mandy Hale, *Beautiful Uncertainty* (Nashville, TN: Thomas Nelson Books, 2014).

[30] Martha Graham, "An Athlete of God," NPR (January 4, 2006), under "Special Series: This I Believe," http://www.npr.org/templates/story/story.php?storyId=5065006.

[31] Stephen Schwartz, "Defying Gravity," *Wicked (Original Broadway Cast Recording)*, Idina Menzel & Kristin Chenoweth, Decca Broadway, 2003, MP3.